DEDICATION

I dedicate this book to my first-born Benjamin Alexander Barnes, words can't express my love for you.

May you inherit a passion for financial literacy and wealth building and spread it like wildfire.

Ben is the founder and co-owner of a small community bank branch.

Ben grew an interest in money at an early age.
Like most children,
he wanted money from his parents to purchase toys and video games.
One day, Ben's dad showed him
how he could grow his money in the stock market
or **by** placing it in an interest yielding savings account.

As a teenager, Ben began to invest in the stock market,
and he even helped older relatives with their stock portfolios.

Ben went off to college with an academic scholarship and
attended a Historical Black College.
While there, he studied finance and economics.
Ben was also a star athlete in college on the basketball team.

After graduation, he pursued a Master of Business Administration (MBA) degree at HARVARD UNIVERSITY.

While Ben attended graduate school,
he was offered an internship at an elite investment bank.
The investment firm trained Ben,
and he excelled above all the other interns.
The senior manager and other employees
noticed his unique zeal for investing.

Ben completed his MBA degree and was offered jobs
at four different elite investment banks.
He accepted one of the offers
and was thrilled to step into his new position as a junior investment banker.
As a junior investment banker, his job was to help companies
and government entities obtain financing,
manage investments, and
act as a financial advisor to individual clients, among other things.

Ben was promoted to a senior investment banker.
However, Ben had a strong desire to help his community and
provide the funding his community desperately needed.
He spoke with his friends from college and his brother Franklin, and
they agreed to form a community bank.

Ben quit his job and opened a bank branch "Freedman's Bank"
with the help of his business partners.
The bank specializes in helping people
from the community obtain homeownership,
small business loans, and capital for community development.
Ben has never been happier in his career.
He enjoys changing the lives of people.

The first banking branch was so successful
that several other branches were opened.
Ben and his partners were able to provide employment opportunities
and teach people about investing money to grow their wealth.

The End

The History of Black Banks

Black owned banks at the peak between the late 19th century and early 20th century had more than 130 institutions operating and providing capital to black enterpreneurs and homeowners during a time when it was very expensive or entirely impossible to get loans anywhere else for blacks. These Banks were mostly in the South. As it stands today in 2019, there are only 19 black-owned banks in the United States. Although the numbers are declining rapidly, with your dreams, expertise and education we can spur the growth of black-owned banks again.

Vocabulary Words:

1. Invest- the act of committed money or capital to an endeavor with the expectation of obtaining additional income or profit.

2. Internship- the position of a student or trainee who works in an oganization sometimes without pay to gain work experience or satisfy requirements or qualifications.

3. Founder- one that establishes an organization.

4. Interest- money paid regularly at a particular rate for the use of money lent or for delaying the repayment of a debt.

5. Capital- the wealth, whether in money or property, owned or employed in business by an individual, firm, corporation, etc.